ISCHEMIA
Restoring Flow

KRISTA HAMMERBACHER HAAPALA

For more information on *Ischemia: Restoring Flow* or to book an event, visit kristahaapala.com.

Designed by D. Grelck

Published intergalactically by 39 Revolutions Press

Printed in the United States

1 3 5 7 9 10 8 6 4 2

ISBN: 978-1-946876-22-5

First printing: January, 2021

Ischemia: Restoring Flow
by
Krista Hammerbacher Haapala

table of contents

right hemisphere

corpus callosum

left hemisphere

For you, human,
as you accept
your magic shines brightest
in the darkest of times.
May you explore and
align and flow with
the emotional physics
of your universe.

Mindfood
(compliments of other heretics)

"The pain was like a wall I had walked through to come out the other side."
~Marina Abromavic

"Artist activity, for its part, strives to achieve modest connections, open up obstructed passages, and connect levels of reality kept apart from one another."
~Nicolas Bourriaud

"I tautologize. I curate. I sociologize. I manifestly manifest."
~Marcel Broodthaers, *My Rhetoric*

"Authentic love must be founded on the reciprocal recognition of two freedoms . . ."
~Simone de Beauvoir

"Once we open up to the flow of energy within our body, we can also open up to the flow of energy in the universe."
~Wilhelm Reich

"The only way I would ever know where to draw the line was by going too far."
~Betty Anne Dodson

~kahh

Preface
A Remarkable Story of an Unremarkable Now

Sitting here on a Monday letting the dark settle in around me. It's the last Monday I'm forty-four. It was a productive day: I did laundry, washed my sons' bedding, and made one of the beds again. My older son, a man as of January, asked me to leave his bedding in a pile on the bed, he would make it. My younger son headed out on a celebratory drive with a friend now that Maine law allows them to drive while they ride in the same car. I also did work for Beacon our gym, cooked dinner, danced, sang, gave my demanding cats the treats I taught them to request with a mew (much to my own newfound dismay), and wrote, including a blurb for a dear one's novel. My love, just back from our gym, is downstairs listening to a podcast about neuroplasticity while doing therapy. Since his strokes due to moyamoya and corrective brain surgery, he does therapy almost every day.

None of this is remarkable. This is my life.

What is remarkable is the tremendous ease I feel in this now. In fall 2016, Brian, my beloved, started having headaches that we learned were transient ischemic attacks, mini-strokes. They were mini, until they weren't. I observed Brian as he walked downstairs at the gym with his left foot dragging and a facial droop; a trip to the hospital diagnosed a migraine. Later that week, working from bed he struggled to talk. I couldn't move fast enough to get him back to the hospital in that terrifying moment with even darker moments to follow.

After what I feel was inordinate medical obfuscation, we learned from Brian's life-saving neurosurgeon during acute circumstances that he needed a cerebral bypass to survive. Due to the use of necessary blood thinners during his first surgery, this inescapable brain surgery had to wait a minimum of seven days. I was informed to bring our sons to the hospital to "spend some time with Dad." What they didn't do was finish their thought: "just in case." What followed were more strokes accompanied by paralysis, then a

wildly successful restoring of flow to Brian's brain, and an un-
deniably altered life for all of us.

The dark has now settled in around me with serenity and elegance
only Mama Nature can create; my computer screen, a portal to all of
you absorbing this remarkable story of my unremarkable now.

I remember the dark rushing in unexpected and devastating, or so I
thought. That deepest darkness brought the most dazzling dawn.

Ischemia: Restoring Flow is a celebration of dark and light, of cata-
strophe and triumph, of paralysis and movement, of surviving
and thriving, of blockage and flow. It takes inspiration from the
gray matter in your skull that is a miracle. We are both
puppet and puppet master. We have the capacity to shape our
brain magic. It's brain magic that made these words, my
choices, your choices. Synapses, hormones, thoughts, intentions;
your brain is a miracle. May you use it in heretical connection
and passionate service of humanity, dear one.

~kahh, The Edge, 3.25.2019

The Neurological Structure of This Book

Ischemia: Restoring Flow is an ugly book. Like the disembodied brain floating in preservative on a disused laboratory shelf, it draws attention, not because you want to look, but because you find yourself compelled, you must. These poems grew out of waiting in hospitals, desperate anger at my love's odyssey in cars before heading home to my boys, sitting with Death as a companion. Even the celebratory poems seemed to asphyxiate upon being committed to paper. What was represented as the ladder out of chaos became a destination where the air was too thin to breathe. Instead of breathing, I wrote and it sustained me, for a time.

The right hemisphere of this book is the place where I have decided the most Stygian of the poems will live: the words written in the depths of ischemia, in lack of flow. In many ways I'm so grateful the injury to my beloved's brain was just so. Damaged in precisely the way that he needed for his Becoming and reconnection to self and life. The uniqueness of his experience is only for him to know, yet I feel the need to share the reflections titrated through my brain as his brain began to heal.

The corpus callosum is the bridge between the hemispheres, the structure evolved to allow integration, connection between the ugly and a more hospitable poetic atmosphere. This bridge is the poem, "grace," in its entirety. My indecision about displaying it in this way is the sole reason this book took vastly longer to take shape than intended. Without this bridge, the leap to the left hemisphere would be too cavernous.

The left hemisphere is still a gaudy, bloody affair, but broadcasts a bit of hope in spite of itself. When your normal becomes an ostentatious affront to equanimity, the words can get ahead of themselves. And then you attempt to logic your way out of the emotional depths. Let me save you the trouble: It will not work. You have to feel your way out. That is an unavoidable, radical truth Jim Morrison shared with us: "You feel your strength in the experience of pain." Upon feeling stronger, the left hemisphere took shape.

These words found their way through me to the pages of *Ischemia* indeed restoring flow. I don't know just why. As Edna St. Vincent Millay reminds us: "Life must go on; I forget just why." It seems trivial to contemplate these words without also considering the whole of life as it carries us on. Bodies, brains, and breath afford us all the opportunity to discover our own why.

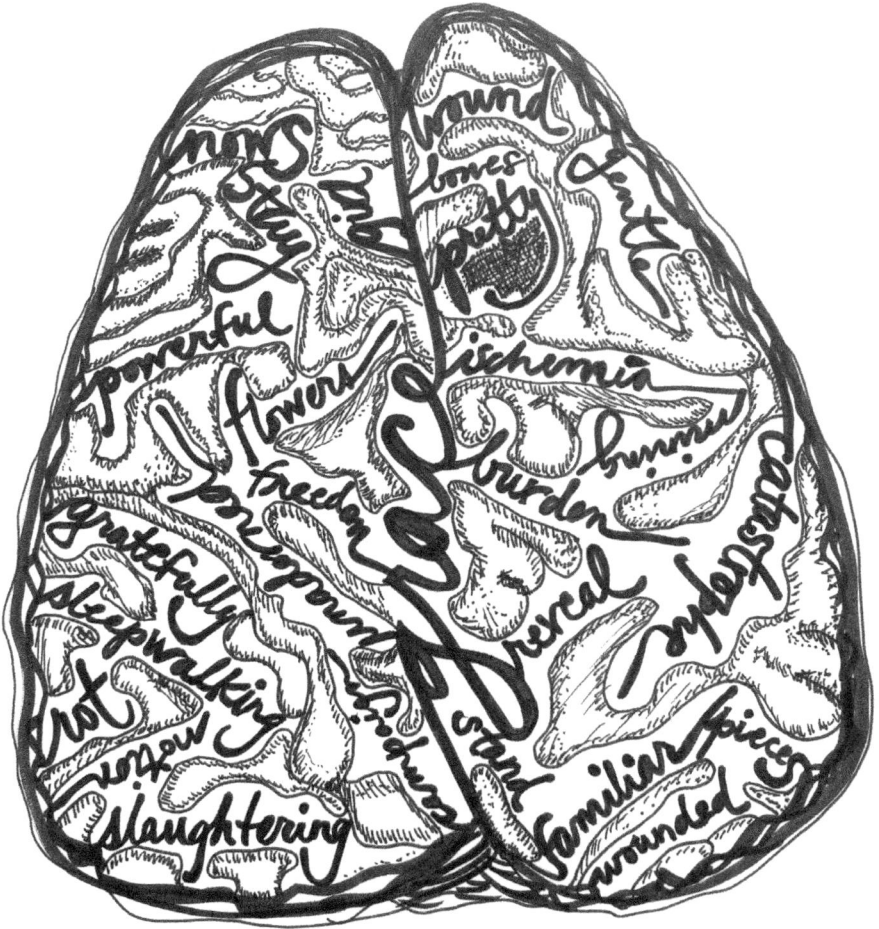

The Angiogram

~kahh

right hemisphere

~kahh

gentle

Days of sweat,
poetry,
heartbreak,
and mundanity,
a suspect grip
on what you
feign as
sanity
leads you into
the backward scene,
a fevered,
painful
Dali dream.
It all seems
right to you,
yet still
the gentle
must opt out
at will.

~kahh

familiar

There is nothing.
(Or) else.

Incapable of pretending,
I ride my reputation
through the town square,
naked,
and sleeping somehow.
Bleeding all
over myself.

offensive

gruesome

female

Before and again,
open to invasion.
Knowing it will be
familiar again.

~kahh

6

wound

Ration your Plath.
Never look into the sun.

As you make the bed,
hold onto the seed.
Regardless of your
frivolous need
to put words together to
make something real.
No one is here
to bother to heal
the wound of the muse,
so useless and crude.

There is work to do here,
children to rear.
The huntress muse
is the least
of my fear.
Despite my drive
to kneel and revere
this gift that
flows
through.

If they only knew
the compelling so true.
Bury it deep
or forgo sleep
until the demons come.
Then you serve none.

Ration your Plath.
Never look into the sun.

~kahh

pretty

Blunt force trauma.
Rape.
[And scene.]

No one here
to share this dream
of a life
so pretty,
when real,
so dirty . . .
the other cheek
when Memory hurts.
Then the shiny,
empty goddess flirts.

Floating through,
she smiles for you.
That girl is no longer
who craves a life
without the waves.
In fact, she brutally
misbehaves
and refuses to sign on
at your behest:

So much better
just to cover
the mess.
No one here
to claim distress.

Tell the walls,
the sky,
the moon.

Never share with those
too soon,
if you wish to fall
in love,
unless
you plan to mourn
severed
connection, access,
expect the infection,
the abscess.

ischemia

As ischemia still
slides around in my brain,
there is wonder

why do this.

Why do these words come?

Just hide and sleep,
your soul to keep.

The fire seems to be
lapping at the pages
of late.

Comfort when
the words don't feel
swollen, bloated
with the expectation
of being
siphoned through eyeballs
and into a mind.

Poetry is a punishment
in high school,
remember?
Yet everyone writes
their own
in the dark.

Haunted.
Haunted
by what

is beyond flow
about this ischemia.
About all ischemia.

This break,
this space,
this massive place
that terror lives
in my head,
so intricately
steeped in dread.

I carry on
in the quiet,
within me
carried by
the perfect
riot.

This adolescent
scheming
has me dreaming
of Cobain,
Morrison,
Dodson,
de Beauvoir,
and Millay
sipping absinthe
around a table
furiously attempting
to label
the genre of their
particular madness
until Plath
walks in and
brilliantly has

this plan
to create a ritual
to invisibly
elevate
the spiritual lace
that adorns
this life they had
that we now
treat as a sad,
incessant universe
we've been
sentenced
to endure.

When all
they
want
is
reincarnation
so they may
hurt, breathe,
and love
in liberation.

~kahh

catastrophe

The only inhabitant
of your love's body
is the phantom left.
After strokes,
brain surgery,
you recognize
the full effect
of the catastrophe.

Unfair
to notice
yourself
in that moment.
You can move,
work,
play.
He struggles to move,
feels the pain,
endures the scars.

And yet
you
need
him.
You
need
him
to evict the phantom,
smile his smile.
But it is not
about you.

The stranger

living within
your love
is not the darkest
part of the catastrophe.

The deepest
darkest,
heaviest,
starkest,
is looking Death
in the eyes,
having no answers.

A solution.
The mere existence
of a solution,
miraculous.
The experience
of the solution,
a miracle.

Recovery is the
gift that animates,
morphs.
A marvel,
a grind,
he perseveres
sublime.
Every day.
Every moment
he is relentless
despite this new
bewildering reality.

There is more
intimacy

than ever before
when you are
each flayed down
to the survival
instinct.

The intimacy of catastrophe
is an irreversible enterprise
resulting in lives
forever entwined.

In this intimacy
we learn
each other anew
letting loose
any grasp
of the past.
It ruins me
from the inside
to look back.

And every particle
of energy is required
for our recalibrated vision,
to remain steadfast.

~kahh

pieces

Dark cutting.
Raw open empty
mind
jutting
into the oblivious
reality
the totality
of insanity
to resume,
presume
your pain,
just vanity.
Your suffering
irrelevant,
your emotion
extravagant.

The idea
you will survive
nothing are the
remnants
of a lucid dream
disintegrating
with consciousness.

Most do not hear
pain.
The tone is
rippled.
It brings with it
an unwanted pressure
for action.
Few take

the next step.

Let the vibration
decompose you.
Your pieces
feel nothing.
Pieces
feel nothing.
Nothing.

reveal

She's rarely
beautiful,
unusual,
an inscrutable excuse
on her lips.
Reading meaning,
conceding
the necessity
of sabotage of her
higher bleeding.

Motionless
in fast-forward,
more words.

She learns
that equanimity
only floats
if it's real.
There's no way
to steal the work
from the future,
no way to cut
a deal.
Only fleshly
slices
slash
the prices.
Only pain accompanies
her grand reveal.

~kahh

mining

Something shifted,
something changed
me
that day.

An irreversible transmutation
from particle to wave.

One cannot unknow when
you
become disposable.

When their treasure
hunt within you
becomes fruitful,
they will
dig
claw
gouge
along the wide,
abundant vein of gold.
Mining
until their
carts are full,
until their
hearts are full,
undeterred,
limits unheard.

Weighed down
with treasures,
they celebrate together
their random

good fortune.

The vein depleted,
the ego defeated,
creates final
recognition
of the
distortion
unheeded.

burden

Annihilated.
Blindsided.
Used.
Deceived.

Thank fuck
it happened.

Being non-consensually
complicit
in inauthenticity
still eats you
from the inside,
you just don't understand
why.
There is a static,
a restlessness,
corroding your identity.

You wonder
what is so difficult
about truthtelling
when that is how
you live
your life.

It's only
in the annihilation
you remember:
trust at your own risk.
Even the most
earnest-seeming humans
will unleash their reservoir

of destructive resentment
they so industriously
garnered and guarded,
then the flash flood
of righteousness,
blindsiding.

A clean sweep
of any positivity
is what they seek,
feeding on the suffering,
using,
because that is
exactly their entitlement.
They will never stop
knowing in their reality
that everything that
created their resentment
is your fault
despite the fact
that resentment can grow
only when
there is no communication.

You have been,
deceived,
forbidden to try.

It is easier
for them that way,
so they can
avoid bearing
the burden of growing.

Leaving their
sterility

in the past
serves the rebirth
from your destruction,
the gift
you can claim
from those unwilling
to grow.

~kahh

stand

When you let someone
stand on your back
to get a better vantage,
a better vantage
of their future,
a better vantage
to what they want and need,
they will either climb off
and lend you a hand to stand
or leave you prostrate
to step directly
on the next back they see.

~kahh

bones

"Good work if you can get it."

"Why the second shelf and not the first?"

They talk past each other
like every other day.
Today, it hurts.

It is good work.

The first shelf is warped
so the mugs don't sit right.
Maybe just use it
for the plates.

"Is there a window open somewhere?"

No.
That's the melancholy
in your bones.
A sweater will just hold it in.
In your bones.

It's a faraway sound,
the sound of a resilient love,
a weather-washed love.
Unremarkable in its persistence
as habits live their own lives.

You get used to
the doing.

You get used to
the quiet.

Sharing the air becomes good enough.
Good enough is hard to leave.
Unless you remember to truly breathe.

"How did you sleep?"

"You know..."

Yes, I know.
I know.
But it is okay for you
to surprise me.
Speak that mindvoice
from the past
that I imagine.

"It's so quiet.
Did you notice?"

"No.
Is there a window open somewhere?"

wounded

What and how
are secondary
to the feelings.

Live in the emotion.
Stand in the fire.
That's what it is.
Standing in the fire.

She stands in the fire
so often
there is nothing
to burn.

But it is gruesome
before the ash,
repulsive;
flesh peels off,
then is incinerated
before their eyes.

They inhale her particles,
her pieces.
They have her within
until they regenerate.

The motherline.
The motherline.
I have furthered
the motherline.
Truncated,
isolated,
I stand alone,

armor on,
in front
of my progeny.

That is where I have landed
with the deaths before me.
I am
the maternal standard holder.
I did not ask for this.

Death and emptiness.
Death comes smoother
to the empty.
Minimal investment.
Minimal impact.
Minimal absorption.
Maximum output
feels the best.
A light unto oneself.
Be a light unto oneself.
Be a light onto oneself.

Embody the ashes.
Embody the clashes.
She will show up for me.
They did blow up for me.

A goddess wounded.

corpus callosum

~kahh

grace

I counted your breaths on Mother's Day

I.

I just want to be able to breathe.

I knew.

I felt…I felt…I felt rotting from the inside.

I knew once I was in your hands I'd be fine.

My girls are strong.

You're here!

I'm so happy you're here.

I just wish I could breathe.

I love you.

II.

The clarity is
undeniable

I am transformed
in your surrender

Your grace

leaves no
work for me

III.

I felt it and decided already.

Is this going to cost a lot of money?
No, Mom, your job is to relax and be here with me.
We have that all set, okay?
Okay.

This means if your heart stops you want us
to do nothing.
Yes, nothing. Wait...
Those coughs suck. Deep as you can, Mom. Use that
oxygen.
Breathe as deep as you can...take your time, Mom.

This means if you stop breathing you want us
to do nothing.
Yes, nothing.
"Sign here."
Kasey, what is the date?
May eleventh two thousand thirteen, Mom.
"And sign here."
What is the date, Kasey?
May eleventh two thousand thirteen, Mom.
"And sign one more time here, Barbara."
It's Barb.
"Sorry. Of course, Barb."
Hey, Kasey, what is the date?
May eleventh two thousand thirteen, Mom.
This is right, right Kasey?
Yeah, Mom, you did great.

Your signature is always so pretty, Mom.
What else should I sign, Kasey?
That's it, Mom.
You did everything you need to do.
You are all set to relax.
So it is done and done? Wait...
Let's sit you up a bit, Mom.

"Does she want a breathing treatment?"

No. Please leave us. Now.

Take your time, Mom. Focus.
Think about touching my hand.
You are here with me. We're together.

Okay. What do I sign so it is a done deal?
You took care of that, Mom, thank you.
Awesome job.
I believe you. I'm relaxed now.
I knew you would take care of me.

IV.

You said
you are ready

Please know
you can go

The warmth of
your hand is
just for me
right now

~kahh

I smile
knowing you
dozed off to
Verlander pitching

V.

Can I go home?
We're going to do what the doctors say, Mom.

Are you okay?
Of course. I'm just happy to be with you, Mom.

I love you.

Who is that?
Just somebody who doesn't need to bother you.
I sent them away, Mom. It's okay.

Why is my doctor Ben Affleck?
Because you totally lucked out!

I'm going to sleep now.

Is it night or day?
It is evening, Mom. The sun is going down.

I want to breathe.

Thank you for the chips, Kasey.

Let's eat our chips.

Who brought these Yellow chips?
I did, Mom. Let's share.

VI.

The first minute
Mother's Day
midnight
floating hands
reaching for
a vision

I'll see someday

The sacredness of
every breath is
stark when
they are numbered

I counted your breaths on Mother's Day

Our breaths
are numbered
between
our first and
our last

Always

VII.

The schedule today is silly.
Yeah, Mom? What's the schedule for the day?
No one needs one anyway. They should think.

What are you looking at, Mom?

I'm just thinking about how beautiful everything is.
The sunrise too.
That window is clear and I can see that...
...that sun...what if it sets?
No matter what, you'll be okay, Mom. Feel my hand?
No. Where?
I'm holding your hand right here, Mom. It feels nice.
Yes. Hold my hand. You're so pretty. I was pretty. You look like me.
Yes, I do. That makes me smile, Mom. I see you in the mirror.
You always will. That's funny, huh?
Take your time. Breathe as deep and you can, Mom. Use that oxygen.

What's after this?
What do you want after this?
Nothing... The beauty.

I'm ready for this to be a done deal.

Don't be sad and don't worry.

Don't be sad and don't worry.

I know you want to be here, but it's not meant to be.

Please leave. Please go now.

I love you, Mom. Thank you, Mom. I love you.

I love you. You go now, Kasey. Go.

VIII.

Leaving
numb
not sad
because Mom
told me
not to

IX.

When your mother dies
you instantly become wiser

She made you
and if you choose to
release her
and then
receive her
her wisdom is for you

All that came before is
consumed and metabolized to
make room for the
grace
to happen

~kahh

left hemisphere

~kahh

unadorned

There comes a time when you
no longer need to be seen.
You see yourself so clearly,
in such stark relief
no other gaze would lend
truer information.
Other perspectives serve
no purpose.

You learn you.
You know you.
You simply are *yourself*
unadorned.

Not the self you grew up being.
Not the self reflected by degrees
or other framed papers.
You are not that self
in the press releases
or the newspaper clippings
on some refrigerator.
Even Google tries
to know you and fails.

You are no longer the catcalled self
or the public speaker self,
not the healing self
nor the entrepreneurial self.

Even those selves so triumphant,
so puffed up with ego:
no valedictorian,
no homeowner,

no professor,
no author.

You are not her.

You are not even
the daughter self,
the mama self,
the partner self.
Although those may be
the closest reflections,
they still shimmer with
the sheen of accomplishment.

There are times though,
there are moments,
breaths you take
as pure love,
as only connection.
Glimpses of the potential
you are when
your inward gaze is untainted,
your outward gaze is only
seeking ecstatic human connection.
The Self that not only remembers,
but also acts according to
the knowing that the sacredness
in each of us binds us
whether our egos
acknowledge it or not.

A heart of fire
burns within each of us
to keep each other warm.

I see myself clearly,

in such stark relief
by the light of my own fire.

In my forty-fourth trip around the sun,
I do indeed love what I see
because my practice is
to dismiss ego,
embody loving connection.

What I don't see is perfection.

What I do see is a fire so relentless
in its love for the world
it has burned away everything
with which I adorned myself.

I am plain,
lucid love,
coherent connection.
I embody my practice,
I stand in Self
unadorned.

~kahh

nows

Love hides
your mind.
It seamlessly
binds
before thoughts
to entwine
remind you
this kind is
a silent find.

It arose.
It grows.
So clear it shows.

Who then knows?
When to expose?

And so it goes.

When they all see,
it seems to me
that everything will
feel so free.
Perhaps it is risk
that is the key.

Forever is
of nows comprised.
Time for the real,
the undisguised.

How real though is advised?

Real enough to
dissolve into
infinity
before their eyes.

slaughtering

Slaughtering Aidos
with my bare hands
relishing unleashing
my brutality.
She has restrained
my progress,
standing in my way;
tall, wide,
endowed with
the strength
I have willingly given.
From a space
of pure folly,
I offered up
my future triumph
for her to sustain
her effortless robbing
of my lifeblood.

No more.

Her eyes are first.
Digging fingers
into sockets.
She screams,
grabbing at her face,
falling to her knees,
blood pooling
where her hands
then meet earth.
Where her blood flows
all growth dies.

No more.

I kick her over
in her agony
hungering to see
the grimace
of fresh blindness.
In her empty
crimson gaze skyward.

I sense Aidos
calculates her fate.

Grabbing her hair,
I drag her
closer to the fire.
Her futile struggle
makes me laugh
violently
remembering
all the times
she and I wrestled
before,
her besting me
every battle.

No more.

Weary,
brushing
my sweat-soaked hair
from my face,
I turn into the heat.
The flames leap
into the dark
seeming to be

anticipating her
grudging sacrifice.

Amid my torrent
of indiscriminate blows,
she acknowledges
my rage.
Through remnants
of teeth she sighs,
"I know. I know.

No more."

Her capitulation
triggers my ceasing
but not my compassion.
She has stolen
too much of me.

No more.

With conviction,
exhaling in
unfathomable relief,
I roll her
massive, limp body
into the flames
to watch her burn.
Noticing her
instinctually resist
as I always had before.

No more.

~kahh

stay

This day
there is
surrendering,
suffering intimate.
And yet I am
already initiate
to Death's breath,
his holy presence.
Both fighting, inviting
this sacred reverence
for the birth,
the waking divine
from this illusion,
this dream sublime.

This day
we surrender
to our knees,
fully human all
in tortured peace,
reckoning with all that is
knowing that this path is his
and Death's together
for the deal:
Will breath cease
or is the path to heal?

This day
is energy,
is spirit,
is portal.

This day

is depths,
is real,
is mortal.

This day
we live
Death visits,
then turns away
allowing
my sun and stars
to stay.

rot

Entropy is an
undeniable
touchstone.

We wail and rail
and punch and fail
to resist
the rot.

Creation of words,
together,
the splendor of
pleasure.

Time begets time,
you know the crime.
You distract yourself
with the sublime lie
that good behavior
earns you blue sky.

Your half-life may
leave you distraught,
but do not give it
another thought.

All
unpredictable,
ruthless,
unsought,
from jackpot to
blood clot.

~kahh

flowers

I have difficulty teaching

boys

the lament of   the world.

The sin-eaters smell of flowers
and death
and are content.

It is when I channel least
I am most
spent.

The world seems clear   no fog   no
clouds

until the plan screams aloud.

When only the sin-eater
can metabolize
what bodies   brains   hearts
attempt to categorize

as that which is forbidden   unsightly   unsaid
until bodies   brains   hearts
are blissfully dead.

The reprieve of the lament
the boys

feel less
unless they risk failure
to guess
the toll the vulnerability will take

on   them

to see   the world

through the goddess eyes
for some comfort, for some surprise

for all will find when love abounds
the sin-eaters may cease their merciful
rounds.

sleepwalking

Needs
and skills
and heedless
thrills.

Wander from
the distant hills
to feed upon the
urban speed
as you choke
upon the seed
of attempting the
creative deed.

Imposters slide
through undetected
until the moment
they are rejected
by the keepers of the
glancing pure.
Knowing they will
cause a stir
in turning
human shells away.
Some will go,
some will stay
and try to live
another day.

Yet it seems
needful
to ask why
this existence

is dead and dry.
No juicy life.
Just angst and strife.

The cynical stand
ready to hand
a knife
to those who find
the cause
to borrow
that which may end
their sorrow.
But *that* edge
is just the cheap way out
of the risk to banish doubt
and own all
that spirit means
in each of all
the magic scenes
that make up
the triumphant
tragic story of
the reality-soaked,
ambiguous glory.

The real,
the flawed,
the sinners all
crawl through rules
awaiting the fall.
Until learning
the rules were
codified
by the eternally
unsatisfied.
So the faceless

must condemn
this lust for life
as not for them.
Leaving the ecstasy
for the brave,
those who are
no longer slaves
to the pointless
limiting thought.
Those willing to be
self-taught
to think instead
of sleepwalking
through this
dream-filled,
earthly,
flesh-bound
fling.

~kahh

powerful

The specter of your void
delicately takes my hand,
winding through the dark
and unexpected,
past the raw and wretched
etchings of my doubt.

A figure of my making,
even in the shadow
she is
the opaque shade
of pain.

Our destination
her unlikely gift.

Guiding me now
with a momentum
I blindly resist,
my hand is electric,
its own hum.
The pace surging,
her insistent urging,
I succumb.

With wide open eyes
then I choose
to see you.
The armor cast aside,
the longing satisfied.
I feel you,
built of emotion,
powerful, tender.
I open my heart

ready to surrender.

Now in the final credits.
And always a pretender.

campaign

Subtle bandits
steal your soul
piece by piece,
without ceasing,
for release
from their
indentured servitude
to their
hollow,
desperate mood.
When you share
energy openly,
you would think
they would see
that stealing
is unnecessary.

Yet still
they carry on
stealthily,
grabbing,
poking,
poorly cloaking
the constant
onslaught
of their hunger,
continuing
their selfish
plunder.

While your instinct
toward rejection
seems to afford
you protection,

closing your heart
can never sustain
the ecstasy of
the love campaign.

gratefully

Sidle over,
saddle up,
coked up
fairies run
amok,
insidious
in their
stand up
dreams taking
me apart
at the seams.

All around are
melting words
while messages
sing through
wings of birds.
Swooping,
diving,
assumed
benign,
yet dismantling
my flesh
design.

Eyes turned
skyward
to evade attack
when

feathers fall,
soft and black.

My salvation
seems so
simple now
as all
the creatures
disavow
my fear
within
the paranoia
sleep.
I pray
the void
my dread
to keep.

mouths

slow

and

taunting

haunt en masse
then gratefully
dawn comes
to pass.

girl

Jung taps me
on the shoulder,
"Your shadow is showing.
Good girl."

At first
I attempted
to tuck it in,
even though
I could tell
it turned him on
to see it.

Then as I moved,
stretched,
suffered to try
to hide it,
he reached out,
asking with his eyes,
so I let him touch.
"Like I thought
it would feel:
Slick,
primordial,
hot as fuck.
Good girl."

After he felt it,
I let it be real.
That slick,
hot darkness
and I danced,
slowly at first.

Learning
each other's steps,
we moved
in deeper rhythm,
wildness growing,
unhinged thinking.

There was
my shadow.

We took turns
leading.
We took turns
trying to keep up.

My head thrown back
to the new moon,
I was
slick,
primordial,
hot as fuck.
And alone.

Good girl.

notion

Fleshly paradoxes
and perplexities
straining under
the complexities.

Notice the fibers
from which the
veil is woven
are strands of
wandering genius
and isolation
blinding us from
the conflagration
of her mind,
a pathological find.

A troublesome bind
to notice the find
that humankind
is uncertainty
in motion.

We are
shapeshifters and ciphers,
a startling notion.

All desire
to declare who
we are.

We are
against ego
both
beggar and star.

~kahh

freedom

Avatar sunshine
sheds light on the ego
and the shadow.
With that, it fades.
Burned away by
the electrons and
intention of the light.
The penetrating physics of
the burning.
Pounding charred bones to ash.

Reaching into the embers,
the burning
in suspended animation for now,
closing fists around
the gray, hot, granular remains
of the trauma and wisdom
in helixes and scalpels.
The burning
ends for now,
with purpose
countering entropy.
There is more time
than I remember
with hands full of my ashes.

Interlude for freedom,
not the freedom,
The Freedom
THE Freedom.
It's all happening.
The inappropriate emphasis
on the inappropriate things,

the howling tongue of
the devil who sings
songs of
the burning.

Earth is turning
hands full of ash,
the burning
fire yearning for
the breath full of ash.
Exhaling onto palms,
fire yearning for
the breath carrying ash.

The Angiogram

Acknowledgments with Deep Gratitude

The acknowledgments are always the sunny part of the book, aren't they? When a book is built of fog and storms, it takes some concentration to feel the sun on one's face. Anything else feels like the Prozac version of the truth.

This book was a maelstrom in my life for formidable reasons, so I must acknowledge the passage of time and the magic of healing for liberating from the maelstrom my drive to create *Ischemia*.

I must also acknowledge the constant riptides, whether they humans (a few), professional distractions (many), or my own state of mind (ever-present, yet malleable). It was swimming parallel to the shore that helped me gratefully rid my life of the undertow.

While swimming, there are those who kept watch from shore. Occasionally the waves obscure my view, but I know they are there. My sons accept me as I am in every moment. Their presence makes me strive to be who I am in their eyes. Dad and Cindy love me no matter what. And my sissy, Trishy, feels it all with me. Hugsandkissesloveyoukbye. And Mom, you'll always be a part of me and we can discuss how we feel about that in my heart. Dr. Rob Ecker saved Brian's life alongside Dr. Jim Kirsh. Rob worked his stunning surgical magic. Jim fought the fucking power so I could break my love out of "rehab" against medical advice and bring him home. Meggie and Fleck listened and raged next to me from afar reminding me who I am in all of this. Ali's presence brings a tenderness and witnessing I'm yet not capable of affording myself. Our faux daughters and their lovies are family through and through. Anna and Joe are our people and simply get it: life and love. My life is richer with mindmelding creativity with my brain twinner Dave. I'm grateful for Kate's creative fire and our mutual Five of Swords tarot catalyst. Our Beacon community buoyed us yet again through the intensity and uncertainty, for that my heart is full of love and gratitude.

And then there is Bri, the Brironman, my love, the one who is still here. It doesn't matter how high the waves get, we swim together. Whether he's tapping my ankle or I'm tapping his, we always opt in to swim together.

About the Author

Krista is the author of *Body 2.0*, *Unlearn Moderation*, and *39 Revolutions*. *Ischemia: Restoring Flow* is her third poetry collection. Since 2005, she also has guided humans of every stripe in creating fiercely fulfilling intentional lives and relationships as a consciousness guide and sexologist. She connects with the world through poetry, art, radical pleasure advocacy, and embodied mysticism. Living in Maine a few steps from the woods, she is the mama of two sons and partner to her love, Brian.

Krista welcomes your connection at kristahaapala.com.

ALSO BY KRISTA HAMMERBACHER HAAPALA

Poetry

39 Revolutions: A Utilitarian Poetry Collection

Unlearn Moderation: Mindfood for Heretics

Non-Fiction

Body 2.0: Finding My Edge Through Loss and Mastectomy